Bhaskar Poldas, Angela Jain

Students' Awareness of Climate Change and Awareness Raising Strategies for Junior Colleges in the Emerging Megacity of Hyderabad

Emerging megacities
Dicussion Papers
Edited by Konrad Hagedorn, Christine Werthmann, Dimitrios Zikos, Ramesh Chennamaneni

Humboldt-Universität zu Berlin
Department of Agricultural Economics
Division of Resource Economics
Philippstr. 13, House 12
10115 Berlin

Tel.: +49 (0)30 2093 6305
Fax: +49 (0)30 2093 6497
www.agrar.hu-berlin.de/struktur/institute/wisola/fg/ress
www.sustainable-hyderabad.de

Contact: emerging.megacities@hu-berlin.de

The emerging megacities discussion papers are available at:
www.eh-verlag.de

ISSN print edition 2193-6927

Emerging megacities Discussion Papers are prepared by researchers working on topics in the realm of sustainable development in Megacities of Tomorrow, a research priority by the German Ministry of Education and Research (BMBF). The papers have been peer-reviewed by a board of external reviewers.
Views and opinions expressed do not necessarily represent those of the Division of Resource Economics.
Comments are highly welcome and should be sent directly to the authors.
We welcome contributions on any topics related to Megacities of Tomorrow. Further information on the submission procedure is given at:
www.sustainable-hyderabad.de/emerging-megacities

Poldas, Bhaskar; Jain, Angela

Students' Awareness of Climate Change and Awareness Raising Strategies for Junior Colleges in the Emerging Megacity of Hyderabad

Emerging megacities Discussion Papers, Volume 1/2011

ISBN/EAN: 978-3-86741-826-3

First published in 2012 by Europaeischer Hochschulverlag GmbH & Co KG, Bremen, Germany.

© Europaeischer Hochschulverlag GmbH & Co KG, Fahrenheitstr. 1, D-28359 Bremen (www.eh-verlag.de). All rights reserved.

Cover: Photo "Metropolis", ferendus (flickr). Creative Commons License

No part of this publication may be reproduced or transmitted, in any form or by any means, electronic, mechanical, photocopying, recording or otherwise, or stored in any retrieval system of nay nature, without the written permission of the copyright holder and the publisher, application for which shall be made to the publisher.

EHV

Students' awareness of climate change and awareness raising strategies for junior colleges in the emerging megacity of Hyderabad

Bhaskar Poldas[*][†], *Angela Jain*[†]

March 2011

Abstract

The paper presents the results of a survey (2009-2011) which aimed at the analysis of the awareness level of junior college students regarding climate change (CC) and its consequences. Based on interviews conducted in the emerging megacity Hyderabad, India and on an institutional analysis of the education sector, teaching modules for junior colleges were be developed to augment knowledge on climate change in future generations.

The topic is linked with the research work of the megacity project "Sustainable Hyderabad" (www.sustainable-hyderabad.in) where climate change impacts are being analysed and mitigation and adaptation measures are being developed. The work presented explores communication strategies which target climate friendly and energy efficient lifestyles and consumption patterns. Furthermore it intends to integrate local knowledge and needs of affected groups in the development of communication and participation strategies to make them efficient and to activate the civil society to take self-initiative.

Key words: *Hyderabad, megacity development, climate change, students' awareness*

---

[*] Corresponding author. Tel.: +49 30 3180 5473. Email: poldas@nexusinstitut.de
[†] nexus - Institute for Cooperation Management and Interdisciplinary Research GmbH, Otto-Suhr-Allee 59, Berlin

1 Introduction

The number of cities worldwide is increasing constantly and the size of existing cities as well. Constant and rapid urbanisation is the basic reason for this trend. "By 2030 more than one third of the earth's population will be urban dwellers." (...) "This phenomenon is being spearheaded by so called megacities (urban areas whose population exceeds 10 million), which are expected to number 26 by 2015, up from a mere five in 1975." This global change does not only impact individual countries or regions but the humanity as a whole.

The emerging megacities still offer an opportunity for intervention to undertake preventive measures and plan the urban development strategically. But climate change and changing requirements regarding low emissions also require new forms and ways of communication and participatory processes. As the debate takes place on different levels, the international negotiations have to be linked to local action and the political and governmental level needs to develop strategies in close co-operation with economic and scientific actors as well as civil society.

With their "focus on approaches that take sustainable development as their starting point and that incorporate the ecological, economic and social dimensions of urban development," the German Ministry of Education and Research (BMBF) selected ten emerging megacities from different continents of the globe as part of their research programme: "Research on the sustainable development of mega-cities of tomorrow". (German Aerospace Center 2011) The South Indian emerging megacity of Hyderabad is one of them. The title of this project – *Hyderabad as a Megacity of Tomorrow - Climate and Energy in a Complex Transition Process towards Sustainable Hyderabad - Mitigation and Adaptation Strategies by Changing Institutions, Governance Structures, Lifestyles and Consumption Patterns* – denotes its objectives.

The population of Hyderabad according to the World Gazetteer was 5,533,640 according to Census of India 2001. It was estimated to be 5,911,831 in 2005 and 6,383,850 in 2010. In the list of 48 most populated cities in India, whose population estimates for 2010 are above one million, Hyderabad occupies the 6th place behind Mumbai, Delhi, Kolkata, Chennai and Bengaluru. (Stefan Helders 2010a) According to estimates its population is growing at a rate of 1.25 % per annum. (Stefan Helders 2010b)

In India a major part of the political discussion is about the distribution of charges and resources between different groups of the society (religion, gender, caste etc.). These constellations have to be taken into account in the development of strategies for sustainability and climate change. (Gey et al. 2007) The consequences of global warming exacerbate existing power relation and generate additional dimensions of inequality. (Ott, Winkler et al. 2004) Growing complexity of environmental issues is a challenge for individuals not only in order to understand the problem, but also in order to translate the information into local action. On the national as well as the international level governments claim civil environmental awareness. (Brunnengräber, Walk 2007) This demands sufficient information and knowledge about the relevant issues from civil society in order to understand the necessity of individual action as being important for solving environmental problems.

2 Research plan

This paper discusses the results of a post-doc research project of Dr. Bhaskar Poldas, funded by the German Academic Exchange Service (GAES). The research was started in 2009 with a literature review on the life style dynamics of youth in Hyderabad. To analyse the awareness of junior college students in Hyderabad on CC, quantitative empirical social research was conducted. Two questionnaires, one for a pre-test and an optimised version for the survey were developed and used. After the survey, the 129 interviews were evaluated with Excel and SPSS software. Based on the results of the evaluation, which show the awareness level of junior college students, teaching modules are planned to be developed in consultation with junior college students and lecturers. They will be submitted to the Board of Intermediate Education and to the Commissioner of Intermediate Education, Andhra Pradesh to consider their inclusion into the syllabus of Intermediate course.

Reasons for selecting "junior college students" for the survey

Students are an important segment of the society, especially in India. They are the focal point of the family and the society. There are about 200 junior colleges in Hyderabad and the total number of junior college students in Andhra Pradesh is about 1.5 million. About 0.8 million of them are studying Intermediate 1st year and 0.7 million 2nd year. (Board of Intermediate Education 2010) The total population of Andhra Pradesh as per census 2001 is 76.2 million. (Government of Andhra Pradesh 2011)

It is expedient to educate students about CC as they are still in the learning phase. They are open to all kinds of impressions and influences, unfortunately also for negative ones, and are vibrant in perceiving, assimilating and putting them into practice. The influence of media on them, especially Television, is clearly evident in their imitation of the western lifestyle. Media, which "is considered as an important source of information, education and entertainment", has also been playing a vital role in influencing the youth culture in India. It has brought the world closer to them and poured new life into the saturated media of the country. (Joshi, Asha B. 2009: p. 145) The revolution of media was supported by new technology, new channels of communication/ information and new gadgets through which the youth received the opportunity to access information and entertainment from anywhere in the world quickly. This bridge has drastically shortened the distance between youth in India and rest of the world. The media exercises a strong influence on youth and their lifestyle through commercials in TV. Efficiently supported by the transport of goods through containers into all corners of the world, the supply of branded international lifestyle products like electronic gadgets, clothing, cosmetics and many other items has been made simple. The products shown in the commercials are readily available to be purchased in the shopping malls around the corner. The streamlining of goods transport logistics has created a new consumption culture in India, especially among youth.

Reports about the involvement of students in the movement for a separate *Telangana* State are published almost daily in the newspapers. This depicts their zeal to fight for a cause which interests and affects their everyday life. They want to have a part in decision making regarding the future, they want to have the feeling that they can make a change. This dynamism could be positively utilised to inform them about the rapidly changing climate, its causes and the measures to mitigate its impacts by adapting their habits e.g. energy conservation.

In the educational institutions students learn about the environment and the society around them. This fundament could be used to expand their knowledge with regard to CC and related problems. The existing educational institutions can serve as channels to convey this knowledge to them. Students can also play an important role at home by informing their parents and siblings about CC and ask them also to adjust their habits to save energy.

Selecting school children in the age group 10-15 years was not favoured as there are three different types of schools in Hyderabad with different syllabi. (Compare Infobase 2011) The first group of schools follows Secondary School Certificate (SSC) syllabus prepared by the State Government of Andhra Pradesh. (Central Board of Secondary Education 2011) The next group follows Central Board of Secondary Education (CBSE) syllabus prepared the Indian Central Government. The third group follows Indian School Certificate Examination (ICSE) syllabus prepared by the Council for The Indian School Certificate Examinations which is a private organisation. (Council for the Indian School Certificate Examinations 2011) The chances of accepting the teaching modules to be prepared in the second phase of the research plan were seen to be meagre in case of the last two groups of schools. Since the junior college students follow a uniform syllabus prepared by the Board of Intermediate Education of the Andhra Pradesh State Government, the chances of implementing the modules seem to be better. (Board of Intermediate Education 2011) Therefore junior college students in the age group of 17 to 19 years were selected as the focus group for the research.

After 10 years of school education, students join junior colleges for studying Intermediate, which has duration of two years. In Intermediate they select a combination of subjects which they want to study further at the graduation level i.e., B.Sc., B.A., B.Com. etc. (Board of Intermediate Education 2011) Irrespective of these subject groups, all Intermediate 1st year students have to pass an examination in environmental science. In Intermediate 2nd year no instruction is given in environmental science. Passing Intermediate 2nd year examination makes them eligible to enrol themselves for graduation courses at Universities or in Degree Colleges affiliated to Universities.

3 Literature review

The research was started with a literature review on the life style dynamics and environmental awareness and environmental behaviour of youth in Hyderabad. It has shown that the information on the topic is scarce. To know what students learn in school, text books of school children in Hyderabad on environmental studies (EVS) were reviewed. Preliminary interviews with school teachers, children and lecturers in Hyderabad have shown that the subject EVS is part of teaching syllabus in the school. In some schools students from 8th class and above are given small projects on environmental topics and are asked to collect information on their own and complete the projects.

The following are some of the topics dealt in EVS text books[1] at the school level:

- Transport & Communication
- Safety on the road

---

[1] Kochhar and Seetapalli (2005); Bhanot (unknown); Rai (2005); Agarwal et al. (2009); Krishnaswamy (2006); Madan (2008); Secretary, CBSE (unknown); Purang and Jaisingh (2006)

- Energy
- Understanding eco system
- Natural resources/ preserving natural resources/ sharing of resources
- Pollution/ industrial pollution/ ways of minimising pollution
- Care and protection of environment/ Environmental values and ethics
- Disaster management
- Waste generation and management

The analysis of the EVS topics at the school and junior college levels has shown that fundamental knowledge about greenhouse effects, global warming and CC is missing in the syllabus. Although pollution is explained as damaging to the environment, no information showing a clear link between CO_2 or GHG emission and CC is given. Consequently the information on the impacts of CC and the measures to mitigate them is as well missing. In EVS class the junior college students are given short texts with various topics related to environment and problems in the society and are asked to collect information on their own from different sources, especially internet. Each of them is asked to write a record on the topic. However, they are not asked to examine their own lifestyle or that of a family member whether it is climate friendly. This underlines the need to prepare teaching modules for junior college students to systematically augment their knowledge on CC.

Well in advance before the final examinations are conducted at the end of the academic year (Intermediate 1st), an examination is conducted in EVS. If they fail to score passing marks, they are denied to appear for the final examinations. In general that is the last instruction given to students in EVS. In Intermediate 2nd year no teaching is given in ecological system and environment related topics. Only some topics related to CC are touched upon, for instance, pollution caused due to *Diwali* festival, poverty, Fluoride in groundwater, changes in farming today, Ozone layer, its uses and its protection, energy consumption in household and ways to reduce it, steps to reduce plastic use, floods in urban areas and accidents in oil wells. The knowledge about climate change and the immediate need to tackle it could be conveyed to the students as part of EVS.

The school is playing an important role in creating awareness among students for the environment in which they live. This process is started already in the 1st class through EVS text books and continued till they leave the school after 10th class. Each class from 1st to 10th has the option to follow one EVS text book from among different ones available. Apart from National Council of Educational Research and Training (NCERT) (NCERT 2011) and Andhra Pradesh National Green Corps (APNGC) (APNGC 2011) several other authors publish EVS text books for all classes.[2] For Intermediate 1st year students APNGC has developed a text book. (Prasanna 2006) As reported by students and lecturers in interviews, some junior colleges do not follow this text book but various other texts on EVS topics prepared by different authors. The subject EVS is taught to students continuously from 1st class to Intermediate 1st year. Since schools and junior colleges are already engaged in instructing the students in EVS, they are a good functioning channel which can be utilised to convey knowledge on climate change as well.

Although the topic climate change is not covered in their college syllabus, it is possible that they might be informed about it through media channels like newspapers, radio or television. An analysis of their awareness of climate change as such was essential before designing the modules according to the students' needs. For the analysis of their awareness, finding answers to the following questions was inevitable.

- Are junior students aware of CC at all?
- What does it mean to them?
- What do they learn about CC in school and college?
- Do they know of its impacts?
- If they have knowledge of CC and its impacts, whether they are participating in any events or campaigns related to CC?
- What role does cultural predisposition play in the perception of CC and in opting for climate friendly lifestyles?

To obtain a broad picture about students' awareness on climate change, evidence-based empirical research in which statistical methods are used was necessary. Quantitative empirical social research was the method found suitable for this purpose, as it is based on statistics. With this aim, empirical research was done during 2010 among junior college students in Hyderabad to analyse their awareness on CC.

---

[2] See previous footnote for some EVS textbooks of other authors.

4 Empirical study

During November and December 2009 the author worked in close cooperation with the members of Work Package 3.2. A "Energy Management" of the "Sustainable Hyderabad" project as they developed a questionnaire for a household survey in Hyderabad.[3] The questionnaire of WP 3.2. A was designed to collect information from households in Hyderabad principally on energy consumption, water consumption and their knowledge, perceptions, awareness and attitudes in general, whereas the questionnaire described below was designed to assess the climate change awareness of students.

Before conducting the survey a pre-test was conducted to find out in the first instance what climate change means to students and how grave, in their opinion, is the problem compared to a few other problems in the society. Apart from giving answers to questions, the pre-test enabled the author to interact with students and to prepare himself for the survey which followed thereafter.

Pre-test: The following two questions were asked in the pre-test. The 1st one was asked to find out what CC means to junior college students or what picture they have about it. In the 2nd question 6 problems were listed and the students were asked to grade them by giving option 1 to the most serious problem in their opinion, option 2 for the second serious problem, 3 for the third problem and so on. The pre-test was conducted with 71 students.

1. What does climate change mean to you? (Selecting more options is possible)
    - o It means air pollution
    - o It means soil degradation
    - o It means environmental pollution
    - o It means water pollution
    - o It means more heat waves are expected
    - o It means ice caps in the polar regions will melt
    - o It means glaciers will melt
    - o It means unpredictable farm yields are expected
    - o It means more heavy rains are expected
    - o It means more floods are expected
    - o It means the sea levels will rise all over the world
    - o It means water scarcity is expected

---

[3] As a native of Hyderabad the author assisted in formulating the questions in the questionnaire understandable to the citizens of Hyderabad and translated the questionnaire into the local language Telugu.

- o It means energy scarcity is expected
- o It means ground water depletion
- o It means depletion of Ozone layer

2. Please grade the following problems according to your opinion. (In the scale 1 = biggest problem, 2 = 2nd, 3 = 3rd, 4 = 4th, 5 = 5th, 6 = 6th problem and 7 = smallest problem)

___ Unemployment
___ Price rise
___ Political instability
___ Environmental pollution
___ Climate change
___ Terrorism
___ Any other, please specify: _____

Survey: The questionnaire for the survey was prepared with 47 questions. A total of 129 junior college students out of 38 different colleges in Hyderabad were interviewed in the survey. From the 38 colleges, 31 were private and 7 government institutions. From private colleges, 104 students and from the government colleges 25 students were interviewed. Of all the students 53 were female and 76 were male.

Six questions were included into the questionnaire to know about the cultural predispositions of junior college students towards climate change. It has been noticed repeatedly that in Hyderabad every year citizens belonging to different religions pray or perform religious rituals for rainfall during drought periods.

The biggest Hindu religious trust in the State of Andhra Pradesh "Tirumala Tirupathi Devasthanam" in Tirupathi performs every year in summer *maha varuna yagam* (a religious ritual) to propitiate the Deity of Rain *varuna* to cause Rainfall. (Rediff.com 2010) Similarly Muslims and Christians also pray for rains every year. (Thaindian 2010; Mohammed Siddique 2010) Though these are religious practices, the common cultural predisposition behind them is the thought that the gods have stopped rains for one reason or the other and when they are appeased, they may show mercy and cause rainfall again.

These practices make a way of thinking evident which is based on the philosophies of different religions. The reason behind such practices in case of Christians and Muslims could be the thought of repentance for their misdeeds, in the conception that the Supreme Being is punishing human beings with droughts because of increased Sin in the world and when they show repentance, He might send relief out of mercy. If that is not the case, they could just be appealing for help in their need. It is a common practice among human beings, who have faith in heavenly help, to pray for relief in difficulties.

Hindus perform the *varuna yagam,* with the wish to propitiate *varuna.* In the Vedic religion, *varuna* was the Deity of the sky, of water and of the celestial ocean, as well as of law. In later Hinduism, he is believed to have his dominion over all forms of the water element. The performing of this ritual by Hindus presupposes that *varuna* is either not happy with the humanity because of their misdeeds and has as a reaction stopped rains to punish them.

Apart from that, all three religions mentioned do have the concept of "end times" existing in their respective religions. Among Hindus this epoch is called *kaliyuga,* for Muslims it is the period before *Qayamat* (Doomsday) and Christians understand it as the time of "Last Judgement". They associate human suffering with this epoch and categorise different negative phenomena or trends in the society as its attributes.

To find the views of students on such religious prayers/ rituals, five questions were included in Part I (Questions 12-16). They were asked whether they will help to bring relief (Q 12) and whether they should be continued further (Q 13). In the following two questions (Q 14 & 15) they were asked whether CC is a result of increased sin in the world and whether they consider it a phenomenon of "end times". In the last question in this section (Q 16) they were asked whether they believe that the effects of CC may decrease if human beings become more spiritual/ religious/ moral/ ethical. In questions 12 and 14 to 16 they had the option "I have no belief in such things" apart from the options "Yes/ No/ Not sure". Answers to these questions are important as they show how they judge the impacts of climate change, whether they hold human beings responsible for climate change or not. If they hold Higher Being(s) responsible for climate change, it denotes that they do not hold humans directly responsible for it.

The distribution of the questions in the questionnaire has been designed as follows:

Part-I	Knowledge, Perceptions, Awareness and Attitudes (18 questions)	
Part-II	Energy and Mobility (7 questions)	
Part-III	Energy in household (4 questions)	
Part-IV	Water use in household (2 questions)	
Part-V	Social capital (5 questions)	
Part-VI	Personal information (11 questions)	

Evaluation of interviews

For the compilation and analysis of pre-test and survey data Excel and SPSS software was used. Univariate and multivariate quantitative analysis methods were employed to analyse the data.

Pre-test: The evaluation of the first question in the pre-test "What does climate change mean to you?" has shown that "air pollution" was the most selected option. For 50 out of 71 students surveyed or for above 70 % of them CC means air pollution. The second choice was environmental pollution, as 48 out of 71 students answered that CC means environmental pollution to them. And the third choice was Ozone layer depletion with 44 students opting for it as meaning CC.

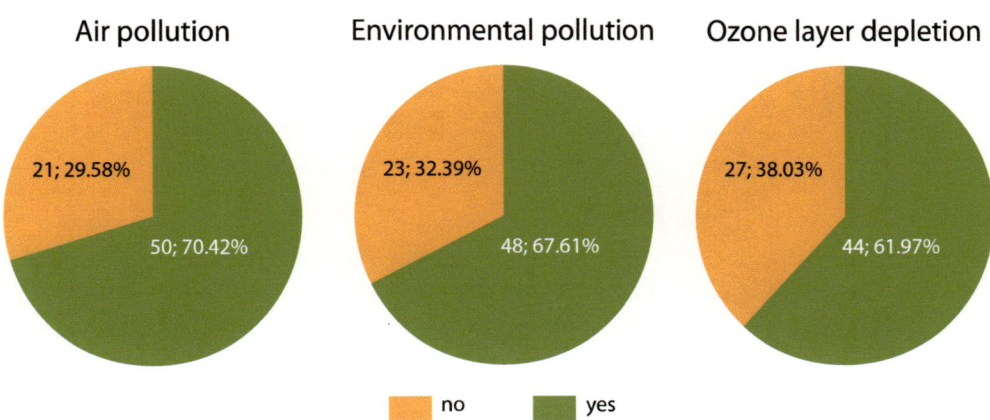

The other options were selected by the students as follows (No. of students):

Water pollution	41
Groundwater depletion	32
The Sea levels will rise all over the world	28
The Ice caps in the Polar Regions will melt	27
More floods are expected	25
More heat waves are expected	23
Water scarcity is expected	23
The Glaciers will melt	22
Energy scarcity is expected	22
More heavy rains are expected	21
Soil degradation	15
Unpredictable farm yields are expected	15

In the second question 25 students said environmental pollution is the most serious problem and only 7 students or 10 % said that CC is the most serious problem.

The answers given to second question are as follows:

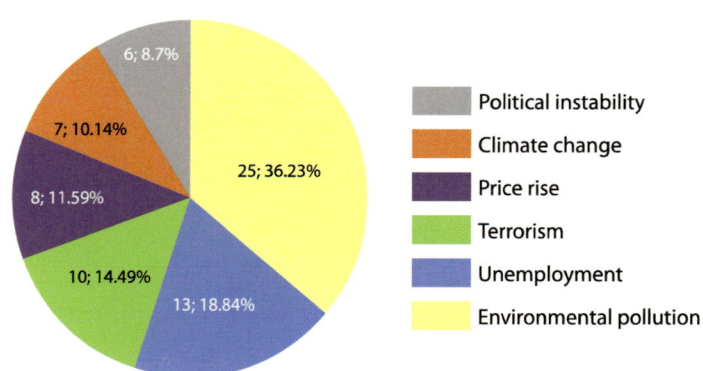

Survey: Few of the survey results are presented below to show how the students have answered the questions in the survey. The first question of the survey was – Where did you hear or read about the following issues? To answer the question the students could make a choice between "never heard", "at school or college", "at home", "from newspaper or magazines" or "from TV/ Radio".

Most interestingly the option "never heard about" was answered as follows:

Never heard about -	No.	Percentage
Global warming	3	2.3 %
Greenhouse gas emissions	12	9.3 %
Increased CO_2 emission is causing global warming	20	15.5 %
Ice caps/ Glaciers are melting	22	17.1 %
Sea levels are rising	21	16.3 %
Ground water is depleting	23	17.8 %
Solar energy	4	3.1 %
Wind energy	12	9.3 %
Rainwater harvesting	17	13.2 %

From the above table it can be seen that the majority of students have heard about the topics mentioned therein. However 12 % of them never heard that "increased CO_2 emission is causing global warming". Above 20 % have mentioned that they have never heard of the impacts of climate change "Melting Ice Caps/ Glaciers", "Rising Sea levels" and "Depleting ground water". It is surprising that the students did not hear about the depleting ground water level, as Hyderabad also experiences this problem every year during summer, especially in the last 5 years. Newspapers carry reports about it. (Siasat Daily 2011) In case of "Wind energy" 12 % of them have mentioned that they have never heard about it and 17 % mentioned that they never heard of "Rainwater harvesting".

In question number 5 the students were asked to mention three causes of CC and give them ranking. Three blank lines were provided under the question for the students to mention the three causes and grade them. This question was asked to test their knowledge about the causes of CC. The causes they mention here would clearly show their awareness level. Some of the possible answers listed really are causes for climate change, but some of them are rather impacts of CC. Out of 129 students who filled up the questionnaires 30 did not answer the question, obviously for not knowing the causes, for otherwise they would not have left blanks. Since the interviews were conducted on college premises in a leisure atmosphere, it can be said that they were not in a hurry to leave blanks. Five of them gave the answer "Don't know", there were 2 mistakes and 92 answered the question. They have mentioned the following factors as the 1st cause of CC:

Factors mentioned as the 1st cause of CC	No. of students
Air pollution	22
Water pollution	10
CO_2	11
Industries and factories	7
Deforestation	7
Environmental pollution	5
GHG emission	2
Lack of awareness	2
Global warming	1
Rise in temperature	1
Chlorofluorocarbons	1
Smoke of vehicles	1
Over use of vehicles	1
Wars	1

Other causes mentioned as the 1st cause of CC	No. of students
Health problems	4
Floods	2
Tsunami	2
Environmental change	1
Rainfall	1
Instable climate	1
Various diseases	1
Instable climate	1
Melting Glaciers	1
Change in sea level	1
Using mobile phones	1
Fires, rockets, blasts in movies	1
Politics	1
Ozone layer decrease	1
Too hot sun	1

From the factors mentioned by the students in the above table it can be noticed that they do not have fundamental knowledge about the causes of CC. Greenhouse gas emission has been mentioned only by 2 students and CO_2 by 11 students as causes of CC. Some of them have mentioned the impacts of CC as causes of CC. The majority of them have heard the various expressions related to CC like global warming or greenhouse gas emissions but they do not seem to have a clear picture how they are correlated. This leads to the conclusion that they have not received proper basic instruction in schools or colleges on CC. The scarce knowledge they posses seem to be limited to hearing or knowing the expressions from various sources. It is a clear indication that the topic CC is not covered in EVS text books.

The answers given to question 17 are shown below:

Climate change is -	Number of students	Percentage
a natural phenomenon	44	34 %
caused by the Sun	3	2 %
caused by man	68	53 %
Not sure	6	5 %
Don't know	1	1 %
No answer	7	5 %
Total	129	100 %

As regards the causes for CC, 34 % of the students have mentioned that the CC is a natural phenomenon. Just half of them said that it is caused by man.

The following questions were included in the questionnaire to know about their cultural predispositions regarding climate change and their views about religious practices for rains conducted every year in Andhra Pradesh. The summary of answers given to them is presented below.

Question	Yes		Not sure		No		No belief		No answer	
	No.	%	No.	%	No.	%	No.	%	No.	%
Will religious practices for rains help?	58	45 %	31	24 %	14	11 %	21	16 %	5	4 %
Should such practices be continued?	47	37 %	47	36 %	27	21 %	–	–	8	6 %
CC is a result of increased sin in the world.	41	32 %	33	26 %	29	22 %	18	14 %	8	6 %
It is a phenomenon of Kaliyuga/ the Last Judgement/ Qayamat.	35	27 %	35	27 %	24	19 %	26	20 %	9	7 %

| The effects of CC may decrease if human beings become more spiritual/ religious/ moral/ ethical. | 42 | 33 % | 33 | 26 % | 25 | 19 % | 18 | 14 % | 11 | 8 % |

From a total of 129 students, 58 or 45 % are of the opinion that religious practices for rains will help and 37 % want them to be continued. About 30 % have answered positively to the next three questions. Most notably, it is surprising to see that 32 % believe that CC is a result of increased in in the world, 27 % consider CC to be a phenomenon of "end times" and 33 % of them even believe that the effects of CC may decrease if human beings become more spiritual/ religious etc. This shows that the percentage of students who believe that cosmic influence is causing CC is quite high. Also the percentages of students who opted "Not sure" to the questions are not negligible.

This kind of belief can lead them to the assumption that human beings are not responsible for CC, but it is being cosmically regulated. If humans are not causing the CC, subsequently it can denote that they also do not need to undertake anything against it, as it is not in their hands. This can encourage them to develop an attitude of apathy towards CC mitigation and adaptation strategies. Most of all to believe that the effects of CC may decrease if human beings become more spiritual/ religious etc. is very detrimental to the campaign against CC, as it shifts the focus away from actively fighting against CC. To work against such beliefs and development of apathetic attitude towards CC, it is primary to educate them on the topic CC.

5 Conclusion

The results of the survey show that junior college students do have some knowledge on climate change and its causes and effects but the answers also reflect their uncertainty and they mix up several topics they have heard of, for example in EVS classes.

The most interesting result is that religion or beliefs play an important role in the view of phenomena which cannot be influenced by the individual directly, like CC. It therefore can be concluded that on the one hand it is crucial to improve the knowledge-base on the topic of climate change and – more crucial – to link this knowledge to habits and everyday life. Another thesis of this paper is that on the other hand the deeply rooted spirituality and religious rituals could be used to change habits and lifestyles, possibly even more efficiently than measures based on rationality only.

Because the above results indicate that junior college students do not have sufficient knowledge about CC based on facts, there is a genuine necessity and an urgent need to develop teaching modules to convey to them the right information on CC, its causes and impacts. Secondly to integrate them into the mitigation and adaptation processes, they have to be educated how they can make a difference by changing their own lifestyles, by playing a leading role in their families in saving fuel, energy, water and by encouraging others to change their lifestyles to become climate friendly.

6 Outlook

Awareness raising strategies

In order to develop strategies for awareness raising and improved learning, it was found expedient to discover answers to the following questions to prepare teaching modules according to the time availability of students and lecturers and to adjust their pattern and standard to students' level of understanding. The questions also focus mainly on the school subject "Environmental Education" (EVS)

- What is the existing opinion about the present study material on EVS?
- What is the opinion about the standard of it?
- How many EVS classes are being held?
- What is the opinion about the existing regular Intermediate syllabus?
- How do they find the idea of preparing teaching modules on climate change?
- How much time could students spend on the proposed teaching modules?

Subsequently, in the second part of the research, two lecturers of two different junior colleges, one principal of a junior college, the Director of Andhra Pradesh National Green Corps and one functionary of the Indian Youth Climate Network were interviewed about the scope of proposed teaching modules. Moreover, a group discussion was also held with three students from three different colleges on the same subject. The aim was to prepare the teaching modules according to the needs of students.

Results have shown that the students do not have enough time to read a lot about CC, because their regular teaching material is too voluminous. They are over burdened with their regular syllabus and would be able to concentrate on new modules only when the volume of existing syllabus can be reduced. The modules should therefore be concise and contain only the necessary information. And linguistically, they should be simple, because the standard of English language among students is mostly low.

Interestingly, in 2006, the Board of Intermediate Education had published in collaboration with Andhra Pradesh National Green Corps, a text book on CC: Intermediate Course 1st year Textbook Environmental Education. (Prasanna 2006) However, most colleges do not use it. Many students do not even know about it. Only government colleges get the book supplied by the government. The students of private colleges have to buy it themselves. But they do not buy it as the managements of private colleges compile short texts on CC and supply them to their students. These texts are meant only to prepare the students for the examination in "Environmental Studies" and not to raise their awareness of CC. The management feels that this examination and the topic CC are a burden to the students. Their primary aim is to prepare the students in regular subjects very well for the examinations and then for the "competitive examinations" to get seats in "medicine" and "engineering" courses. As the number of successful students from a particular junior college at these competitive examinations increases, the reputation of the college goes up. As a result, more students join this college and its management earns more money. That is the prevailing situation.

Preparation of teaching modules on Climate Change

Based on the suggestions of lecturers, students and others mentioned the teaching modules on climate change have been prepared for junior college students in Hyderabad. They have been submitted to the Board of Intermediate Education (BIE), Andhra Pradesh and to the Commissioner of Higher Education, Government of Andhra Pradesh with a request to consider them for inclusion into the syllabus of Intermediate 1st year. The two officials in this regard have informed the authors that the Board will scrutinise the modules and consider to include them into the syllabus.

In the meantime the BIE has announced in the media about its plans to revise the syllabus of Intermediate. The modified syllabus will be effective from the academic year 2012-13. In a report in the local Telugu newspaper – Eenadu to this effect, the Convener of Engineering, Agricultural and Medical Common Entrance Test (EAMCET) also stated that the syllabus volume of physics subject would be reduced, as the students are facing difficulties because of its complexity.

The plan of BIE to reduce the volume of physics syllabus corresponds to the wish of junior college students and lecturers expressed during interviews to reduce the existing syllabus before including more topics. It is therefore conducive to discuss strategies for integration of the teaching modules on CC in the existing syllabi with the BIE at this juncture as the conditions are favourable revision phase.

References

Literature

Agarwal, Poonam/ Agarwal, Ranjana/ Dhamija, Parveen (2009): Pitambar Interactive Environmental Education for Class VII. Pitambar Publishing Co.: New Delhi.

Bhanot, Reinu (n/a): Environmental Studies 5. Golden Bells Publishers: New Delhi.

Brunnengräber, Achim/ Walk, Heike (2007): Multi-level Governance. Klima-, Umwelt- und Sozialpolitik in einer interdependenten Welt, Schriften zur Governance-Forschung, Band 9, Baden-Baden: Nomos-Verlag

Gey, Peter/ Tenbusch, Renate, Jobelius, Matthias (2007): Indien – Herausforderungen auf dem Weg zur Weltmacht. Aus der Reihe: Kompass 2020, FES, Bonn/ Berlin.

Joshi, Asha B. (2009): New Generation Youth Lifestyle and Food Consumption Patterns. In: Monica Rao (Ed.) A New Generation Youth Lifestyle. Influence and Impact. Icfai University Press: Hyderabad.

Kochhar, Geeta/ Seetapalli, Radha (2005): Frank Environmental Education Class 4. Frank Brothers & Co.: Hyderabad.

Krishnaswamy, Ranjini (2006): Environmental Education for Class 8. Madhuban Educational Books: New Delhi.

Madan, R. L. (2008): Saraswati Environmental Education. A Textbook for Class IX. Saraswati House. New Delhi.

Ott, Hermann E.; Winkler, Harald; Brouns, Bernd; Kartha, S. ; Mace, M.J.; Huq, S.; Kameyama, Y.; Sari, A.P.; Pan, J.; Sokona, Y.; Bhandari, P.M.; Kassenberg, A.; La Rovere, E.L.; Rahman, A. (2004): South-North dialogue on equity in the greenhouse : a proposal for an adequate and equitable global climate agreement. - Eschborn: Deutsche Gesellschaft für Technische Zusammenarbeit (GTZ).

Prasanna Kumar, W. G. (Editor) (2006): Intermediate Course 1st year Textbook Environmental Education. Andhra Pradesh National Green Corps.: Hyderabad.

Purang, Y. P./ Jaisingh, Sunita (2006): Environmental Education for Us. Arya Publishing Co.: New Delhi.

Rai, A. N. (2005): A Textbook of Environmental Education for Class 6. Goyal Brothers Prakashan: New Delhi.

Secretary, CBSE (?): Environmental Education Class 9. Central Board of Secondary Education, New Delhi.

Web links

German Aerospace Center (2011) Project Management Agency (PT-DLR): www.emerging-megacities.org/seiten/thematik/forschungsbedarf/forschungsbedarf-en.aspx [18-02-11]

Stefan Helders (2010a) www.world-gazetteer.com/wg.php?x=\&men=gcis\&lng=en\&dat=80\&geo=-104\&srt=pnan\&col=aohdq\&msz=1500\&va=\&pt=aIndia:metropolitan areas [20-07-10]

Stefan Helders (2010b) http://bevoelkerungsstatistik.de/wg.php?x=\&lng=en\&des=wg\&geo=-104\&srt=npan\&col=abcdefghinoq\&msz=1500\&men=gcis\&lng=de [20-07-10]

Board of Intermediate Education (2010), Andhra Pradesh http://bieap.gov.in/resultanalysis.html [07-07-10]

Government of Andhra Pradesh (2011) www.aponline.gov.in/apportal/HomePageLinks/Population.htm [07-03-11]

Compare Infobase (2011) New Delhi: www.indiaedu.com/andhra-pradesh/school/ [09-02-11]

Central Board of Secondary Education (2011) New Delhi: www.cbse.gov.in/welcome.htm [09-02-11]

Council for the Indian School Certificate Examinations (2011) www.cisce.org/SyllabusFor$\_$ICSE2011.jsp [09-02-11]

Board of Intermediate Education (2011) Andhra Pradesh: http://bieap.gov.in/functions.html [09-02-11]

Board of Intermediate Education (2011) Andhra Pradesh: http://bieap.gov.in/general courses.html [09-02-11]

National Council of Educational Research and Training (2011) www.ncert.nic.in/publication/publication_list/pdf_files/textual.pdf [11-03-11]

Andhra Pradesh National Green Corps (2011) www.ngc.ap.gov.in/english.html [11-03-11]

Rediff.com (2010) India news: http://specials.rediff.com/news/2008/jul/23slid1.htm [07-07-10]

Thaindian (2010) news syndicate: www.thaindian.com/newsportal/enviornment/unique-ritual-in-hyderabad-to-propitiate-rain-god_10075014.html [07-07-10]

Mohammed Siddique (2010), Correspondent, TwoCircles.net: www.twocircles.net/2009jun28/tearful_prayers_offered_muslims_rains.html [07-07-10]

Siasat Daily (2011), Hyderabad: www.siasat.com/english/news/ground-water-takes-further-dip [09-02-11]